A CULTURAL JOURNEY THROUGH INDIAN NUPTIALS

DR. JAGADEESH PILLAI

|| *"Dedicated to all who seek to understand and appreciate Indian culture and tradition."* ||

୫

Contents

Contents

PRAYER

**"Om Bhadram Karnebhih Shrunuyaama
DevaahBhadram Pashyemaakshabhiryajatraah
SthirairangaistushtuvaamsastanoobhihVyashema
Devahitam YadaayuhSwasti Na Indro
VridhashravaahSwasti Nah Pooshaa
VishwavedaahSwasti Nastaarkshyo ArishtanemihSwasti
No Brihaspatir DadhaatuOm Shantih, Shantih, Shantih"**

The literal meaning of this mantra is: OM. O Gods! Let us
hear auspicious words from our ears. O reverent Gods! Let
us behold propitious visions from our eyes, let our organs
and body be stable, healthy, and strong. Let us do that
which is pleasing to the gods in the life span allotted to us.
May Indra, inscribed in the scriptures, bring us fortune!
May Pushan, the knower of the world, grant us prosperity!
May Trakshya, who vanquishes enemies, bestow us with
blessings! May Brihaspati bring us success!
OM Peace, Peace, Peace.

ABOUT THE AUTHOR

Dr. Jagadeesh Pillai is a renowned Guinness World Record holder, writer, and researcher hailing from Varanasi, also known as the abode of Lord Shiva. With a Ph.D. in Vedic Science and a range of creative ideas and achievements, he is a true polymath. He is the author of more than 100 books including Research Publications. Although his roots can be traced back to Kerala, the people of Varanasi hold him in high regard and affectionately consider him one of their own.

Dr. Pillai has achieved four Guinness World Records in the following subjects:

"Script to Screen" - In this record, Dr. Pillai produced and directed an animation film within the shortest time possible, breaking the previous record set by Canadians. He has also received numerous national and international awards and recognitions for this achievement.

Longest Line of Postcards - For this record, Dr. Pillai created a line of 16,300 postcards on the occasion of the 163rd anniversary of Indian Postal Day. The event also included a questionnaire about the Indian flag.

Largest Poster Awareness Campaign - Dr. Pillai designed an awareness campaign on the subject of "Beti Bachao - Beti Padhao" (Save the Girl Child - Educate the Girl Child) to achieve this record.

Largest Envelope - In tribute to the Indian Prime Minister's

"Make in India" initiative, Dr. Pillai created a 4000 square meter envelope using waste paper to achieve this record.

Attempted - **70000 Candles on a 210 kg Cake** - To celebrate the 70th Indian Independence Day, Dr. Pillai attempted to light 70,000 candles on a 210 kg cake, which was recorded in World Records India.

Attempted - **Documentary on Dhamek Stupa of Sarnath in 17 Languages** - Dr. Pillai attempted to create a documentary on the Dhamek Stupa of Sarnath, dubbing it in 17 different languages. The result of this attempt is currently awaiting confirmation from the Guinness World Records.

Dr. Pillai is skilled in teaching the Bhagavad Gita, a Hindu scripture, and is popular among young people. He has helped many young people improve their lives through his motivational teachings.

In addition to teaching, he has composed and sung numerous Sanskrit Bhajans and patriotic songs.

He has also written and directed several short films and documentaries for awareness campaigns, and has volunteered with the police in both UP and Kerala to spread awareness about various issues through videos and photography.

Incredibly, he has produced and directed over 100 documentaries about the city of Varanasi, all on his own.

He has also helped and guided more than 25 boys and girls to achieve world records through creative and innovative methods. He is a multifaceted person who uses his intellect and the blessings given to him by God to excel in various areas. He is both a teacher and a student, always learning and teaching, and is able to master any subject he comes across.

He is a selfless social activist and motivational speaker who has overcome struggles and failures to become a successful and enthusiastic individual with a rich life experience.

In addition to his work with the Bhagavad Gita, he is also an efficient Tarot card reader, Astro-Vastu consultant, and a talented singer and composer. He has sung the entire Ram Charita Manas and Bhagavad Gita in his own compositions, and has sung the phrase "Lokah Samastha Sukhino Bhavantu" in 50 different languages. He is currently working on a detailed and scientific study of Vedas, Upanishads, Puranas, and the Bhagavad Gita. He has also composed and sung the Hanuman Chalisa and Gayatri Mantra in 108 and 1008 different compositions, respectively.

Awards - Four Times Guinness World Records, Winner of Mahatma Gandhi Vishwa Shanti Puraskar, Mahatma Gandhi Global Peace Ambassador, Kashi Ratna Award, Dr. APJ Abdul Kalam Motivational Person of the Year 2017, Mother Teresa Award, Indira Gandhi Priyadarshini Award, Bharat Vikas Ratna Award, Udyog Ratna Award, Vigyan Prasar Award, Poorvanchal Ratn Samman.

Preface

This book is a comprehensive exploration of the various customs and traditions of Indian weddings around the subcontinent. It is a delightful account of the various symbols and rituals of Indian cultures, specifically the wedding customs and practices, that continue to be observed to this day.

In this book you will experience the opulent beauty of a dazzling wedding parade, learning about the careful planning it takes to make such an event happen. We will explore the colorful array of rituals and the meaning behind the decorum of the wedding couple and their families. From food to flower arrangements to the specific design of the wedding dress, this book will guide readers through a detailed examination of the many symbolic and traditionally significant elements of Indian weddings.

This book is a window into the numerous charismatic customs and rituals of Indian weddings, each having its own unique meaning behind it. It is an intricate selection of culturally relevant details and tidbits from the various customs from different regions around the subcontinent. This book brings the delightful complexity behind what makes Indian weddings truly unique.

Beyond the rituals and customs, this book also gets at the spirit of Indian weddings. It details the joy, passion and vibrant energy that is present at a typical wedding, showcasing the reason why the occasion is such a memorable and meaningful event in India. In addition to the historical and cultural significance of the wedding, the book captures the emotional connections that are forged between the different members of the families and those around them.

The "A Cultural Journey Through Indian Weddings" is an essential book for anyone interested in the rich culture and history of India. It provides an in-depth account of how the beauty and significance of the Indian wedding works, connecting the many regions of the subcontinent as well as showcasing the vibrant emotions that come with such an event. I am proud to serve as a Preface for this book and I am pleased to see this meaningful exploration of Indian weddings is widely shared.

I

Introduction: Understanding Indian Weddings

The Indian wedding is an important and complex tradition in India and it has roots in India's rich cultural heritage. Indian weddings are steeped in centuries of colorful customs, intricate rituals, vibrant decorations, and festive music and dance. They are vibrant and colorful celebrations, full of meaningful customs that have been passed down through generations. These deeply meaningful rituals celebrate the union of two souls and bring together families and communities, which are a crucial part of Indian culture.

Although each region of India has its own unique set of customs and traditions, Indian weddings generally feature lots of singing and dancing, beautifully decorated venues, delicious Indian food, and the color and beauty of a myriad of diverse cultures. They also often involve a Vedic ceremony known as the "Saat Phera", which is a symbolic expression of the seven promises that the bride and groom make to each other so as to make their new life together as blissful and prosperous as possible.

One of the key features of an Indian wedding is the colorful and elaborate clothing for the bride and groom. The groom usually wears a traditional outfit in colorful, embroidered fabrics such as sherwanis, jodhpurs, bandhgalas, or dhotis. As for the bride, she typically wears an embellished traditional Indian sari, ghoongat, or lehenga. Her hair is often elaborately styled, with garlands made from jasmine, tuberoses and marigolds.

The days leading up to the wedding are often full of customs and ceremonies. In Hindu marriages, the bride's family often hosts a 'Haldi' ceremony, in which a paste of turmeric, sandalwood, almond oil, and rosewater is applied to the bride and groom to purify and bless them. The groom is also traditionally welcomed to the bride's house by her family in the days before the wedding. On the day of the wedding itself, the groom is often accompanied in a procession to the venue and is welcomed by the bride's family.

At the end of the ceremony, the couple is declared "man and wife" and the bride usually departs from her family's home to go and live with her husband's family. And then begins the much needed post-wedding celebrations and festivities, which can often last for days.

Understanding the Indian wedding is essential for anyone

looking to appreciate the beauty and meaning behind this ancient tradition. Once you understand and appreciate the array of rituals, customs, and traditions that make up an Indian wedding, you can not only revel in the joy of the celebrations, but also find deeper meanings about the importance of committed relationships, the transcendence of love, and the celebration of life.

"A wedding is more than just a ceremony; it is a reflection of two souls uniting and cultures blending."

߷

II

Pre-Wedding Customs & Rituals: The engagement & Haldi Ceremony

Pre-wedding customs and rituals are a significant part of Indian culture and are deeply woven into the fabric of Indian society and family life. Traditional pre-wedding ceremonies such as the engagement and haldi ceremony help to bring families together, symbolize the new union and create a sense of harmony.

The engagement ceremony is usually the first step in the traditional pre-wedding ceremonies and marks the acceptance and agreement between the two families to marry their respective sons and daughters. It usually begins with the parents of the groom coming to the bride's home and asking for her hand in marriage. The bride's parents also welcome the groom's family and accept their proposal with an exchange of gifts. After asking for the bride's hand, the groom places a ring on the finger of the bride and they exchange garlands to signify the commitment of marriage. After the exchange of rings, both families are given a feast and blessings by the elders of the family.

The haldi ceremony is the second step in the traditional pre-wedding ceremony and is an important ritual for both the bride and the groom. During the haldi ceremony, turmeric is applied to both the bride and groom as they symbolize the removal of any physical or bad spiritual forces or negative energies. After the haldi application, the entire family gathers and showers them with blessings. The haldi is also considered a symbol of good fortune and having a family member from either side apply it is considered auspicious. After applying haldi, the bride and groom are usually taken for a ritual bath to cleanse their body and soul before the wedding.

The traditional pre-wedding rituals are part of the ancient Indian culture and customs and add to the joy of the wedding event. They represent solemn commitment and signify the new bond that is being created between two families. These rituals are a cherished part of the Indian wedding, and it is essential to follow them as closely as possible, to ensure that nothing goes wrong on the special day.

"May your wedding be as exquisite and beautiful as that of kings and the royal family."

&

III

The Baraat: The Groom's Procession

The Baraat is the traditional procession of the groom on the way to the wedding. It is considered to be the most important part of an Indian wedding and is usually celebrated with much fanfare and joy. It's a momentous occasion, especially for the groom and his family, who often arrive with a procession including relatives and friends, accompanied by music and dance.

The concept of the Baraat is steeped in Indian culture as a way of paying respect to the groom's family. Usually the groom arrives at the wedding site in a horse-drawn vehicle such as an open-top limousine or a jeep. The driver of the vehicle, usually a close relative of the groom, carries a ceremonial sword and holds the reins, while the bride's family members welcome him with garlands of flowers and a shower of petals. A band or a dholi - a traditional Indian drum - is also part of the procession, playing music as the groom enters the wedding venue.

The procession is traditionally led by the groom who is accompanied by his relatives and friends, known as the baratis. These baratis are often seen adorned with bright outfits and jewelry, and may even wear traditional Indian attire. They often dance and sing, making the atmosphere more joyous and celebratory. As the groom enters, the bride's family members greet him with gifts and blessings for a happy married life.

Once the groom has arrived at the wedding venue, he and his family are welcomed with more gifts and blessings. The groom is also presented with a kalire which is an indispensable part of an Indian wedding, as it symbolizes the significance of having a family. The groom then garlands the bride and the ceremony begins.

The Baraat is a vital part of Indian weddings as it celebrates the union of two families and two lives. Apart from being a source of joy and entertainment, it is also a way of honoring the groom and his family. The Baraat tradition is here to stay, as it remains a significant part of the Indian wedding culture and is an integral part of the wedding experience.

"A wedding is a time for the coming together of not only the bride and the groom, but also of two different families."

೫

IV

The Mehendi Ceremony: The Henna Night

The mehendi ceremony, often referred to as the henna night, is one of the most important and beautiful weddings ceremonies in India. This ceremonial event is often held prior to the wedding day, and is meant to bring the bride and groom each good luck, joy and blessings for their future life together.

The mehendi ceremony is a time of celebration, music and dance as family and friends of both the bride and groom gather together to mark the start of the wedding festivities. During the mehendi, the bride is lavishly adorned with henna; a beautiful, naturally occurring dye that is applied to the bride's hands and feet to create intricate and detailed patterns and designs. The bride will typically have a mix of traditional and modern designs created, and the designs often have special hidden messages; the groom's name or family initials are often included in the design so that he knows that the bride he has been waiting for is ready! The mehendi can take many hours to apply on the bride and is a symbol of prosperity and joy for the couple.

The mehendi is also a time for families to socialise and come together, and as day turns to night, dance and music come to life. Traditional Indian music will be played and the bride and groom's families and friends will all join in the dancing. A lot of the Indian wedding rituals will be carried out during the mehendi ceremony such as the giving of gifts to the bride from her family such as saris, jewellery and diamond rings, making it a really festive and joyous celebration.

Upon completion of the mehendi, the bride will take on a striking look as all her hard work and design reaches its fruition. The other members of the party will have also been applying mehendi and often the bride's friends and bridesmaids will surprise the bride with special designs on the back of their hands, linking each other through secret symbols of a life long friendship.

The mehendi is an important part of an Indian wedding, a time when the bride and groom come together to celebrate their pending union. It is a night of joy and happiness as family and friends come together to witness the start of a new chapter for two loving families.

"The many fun and exciting rituals that take place during an Indian wedding, make for an ever-memorable occasion."

&

V

The Wedding Ceremony: The Main Wedding Rituals

A traditional Indian wedding is an elaborate and intricate affair, characterised by numerous colourful ceremonies and rituals. Unique and full of deep symbolism, these rituals vary from region to region within India, with each one having its own cultural significance. The list of traditional rituals that take place during a wedding are often long and complex. The majority of these ceremonies can usually be categorised into pre-wedding rituals and wedding day rituals, with a post wedding ritual also occurring at a later date.

Pre-wedding Rituals

The pre-wedding rituals are incredibly important in Indian weddings, typically occurring over a period of several days. During this time, the families and the couple come together to celebrate and bond. The most important pre-wedding ceremonies are the Rokka, Haldi and Mehndi, which are all full of complex symbolism.

The Rokka is a ceremony conducted by both families, during which the bride's father presents the groom with various gifts known as the 'akhdi'. These gifts symbolise the strength of the bond between the two families. The bride's father also places a specially prepared turmeric paste on the foreheads of the bride and groom, signifying the start of the ceremony.

During the Haldi ceremony, bright yellow saffron haldi paste is applied to the faces, hands and feet of both the bride and groom, along with a few guests from both sides of the family. It is believed to bring good luck and health to the couple and ward off evil.

For the Mehndi ceremony, both the bride and groom have intricate mehndi patterns applied to their hands and feet. This is a celebration for the bride and her female family and friends, who get together to enjoy music and dance.

Wedding Day Rituals

On the wedding day itself, the ceremony is an elaborate and complex affair, with a number of different rituals conducted throughout the day. The most important of these is the exchange of garlands between the couple, known as the Jai Mala. This signifies the acceptance of each other as life partners.

The tying of the sacred thread (saptapadi) is another very important ritual. The bride and groom walk around the holy fire, accompanied by seven steps, each step representing the seven vows made to one another. Later in the ceremony, the groom applies vermilion to the bride's forehead, while they exchange rings wearing fragrant flower garlands around each other's necks.

Post-wedding Rituals

At a later date, the couple's families will come together to celebrate the newlywed's first official gathering, known as the Ghauhar. The bride, along with other female family members, will dress up in beautiful saris and accessories and be presented with gifts from her in-laws. This is a joyous occasion that marks the start of the couple's new life together and is a time for them to receive blessings from their families. The Ghauhar is a time-honored tradition that is celebrated with much fanfare and is a beautiful way to honor the newlyweds.

"An Indian wedding is not just about the ceremony, but a time for both families to unite in celebration."

౪

VI

The Reception: Post-Wedding Celebrations

Indian weddings are truly a magical event that families and friends celebrate together. Once the couple have tied the knot, it is time to celebrate the union with the reception. The reception is a grand post-wedding celebration that is thrown for the newlyweds.

No matter the size of the reception, the wedding from the perspective of the guests is an enormous show of culture and lifestyle. It gives guests a chance to witness a different part of the traditional culture and also some modern practice.

The Indian wedding reception typically starts with a grand entrance of the couple, heralding their union and signifying the beginning of a new life together. The reception includes a one-on-one introduction of the couple to their guests. Known as the garland ceremony, the couple is garlanded, marked with the application of sindoor, the groom's umbrella and kneeling in front of each other. It is a symbol of their love and commitment which is admired and celebrated by the guests.

The evening usually then proceeds with guests being enthralled with entertaining performances. It could quite possibly be anything from a live traditional band, to various cultural performances, to a dance sequence. At a reception, it is usual to find guests dressed in their best traditional attires. Women adorned with heavy Jewelry and men in their wedding finery and gaudy waistcoats.

The food served at an Indian wedding reception is also something to look forward to. One will find the customary Indian cuisine and delicacies prepared, such as Biryani, Roasted Chicken, Pakoras and Sago Ladoos. Additionally, a lot of hotels and venues provide International cuisine, added to give popular global dishes a local touch.

Finally, the events probably culminate with a presentation of congratulatory gifts to the couple. As a general practice, the couples generally thank and greet their guests individually as a show of appreciation. At last, the reception comes to a close with the couple leaving together, signifying togetherness and union.

Reception is a very important and auspicious ceremony that is almost an integral part of any Indian wedding. It is the culmination and celebration of the marriage and ensures that none of the important steps are left undecorated or uncelebrated. The reception marks a new beginning of the newlyweds as they embark on a new journey of togetherness.

"An Indian wedding is the perfect way to celebrate the two families coming together as one!"

&

VII

Regional Variations: North, South, East & West Indian Weddings

A wedding is a commitment and cultural union between two individuals that signifies the start of a new family. Despite being one of the most celebrated and joyous occasions in any culture, a wedding day can differ drastically depending on the location and the traditions of the married couple's family. Indian weddings are characterized by vibrant colors, opulent settings, elaborate decorations, and a variety of ceremonies that range from simple to complex, stretching over multiple days.

Weddings in North India are traditionally grand, taking place in the bride's family home or a large, hired wedding hall. The wedding is typically planned by the bride's family and the menu, music, and decorations have distinctive regional flavoring. The celebrations especially feature the music and dance of the region. The varied rites of Hindu weddings are usually followed with special traditional customs such as Chatt, Suhag, and Mehndi being at the forefront of the celebrations.

In south India, the wedding ceremonies may differ from state to state. According to Tamil culture, weddings are typically held in the morning when the sun is shining. The wedding usually consists of the classical Indian ceremonies like Saptapadi. After the ceremony, elaborate and stunning decorations are made at both the bride and groom's homes and traditional music is played throughout the day.

East India typically follows the rituals of Hindu marriages but with its own regional touches. The wedding customs start with a Sankha ceremony, followed by Shaka, Pani Bharni, Kurmaavatara and Managal Aarti. Symbolizing the groom's entry, a procession of drummers, musicians and dancers then welcome the groom to the wedding venue. Further rituals include exchanging of garlands, lighting of the sacred fire, the tying of the mangalsutra and homams or chanting of mantras to bless the couple.

In West India, the wedding typically takes place in the late evening and follows the Vedic ritual path. Traditionally in Gujarati weddings, a sacred canopy is constructed from bamboo and covered with cloth, which is underneath the mandap where the marital ceremonies take place. Rituals like Jaimala, Pheras, and Kanyadaan are performed as well as traditional Gujarati meals being served.

No matter where an Indian wedding hails from, the celebration is usually full of vibrant colors, mouth-watering delicacies, extraordinary decorations and lots of joy. Indian weddings are celebrated with joyous enthusiasm by family, friends and neighbors and the union of two individuals is seen as the union of two families and two souls.

"The vibrancy and liveliness of an Indian wedding is unparalleled."

☙

VIII

The influence of Religion on Indian Weddings

Religion plays an important role in Indian weddings, as it influences the cultural traditions and rituals that take place during the ceremony. In India, the majority of weddings are presided over by Hindu priests, who lead the guests in a range of religious observances.

The marriage is typically an intimate private ceremony involving the couple and their families, but also includes blessings from a temple priest, who historically was responsible for conducting marriages. The rituals attached to a traditional Hindu marriage reflect the importance of the bond between two people and celebrate the fundamental building blocks of any successful relationship – companionship and partnership.

In India, the wedding is based on the ancient Hindu scriptures, particularly the Rigveda. The scriptures provide the framework for the wedding ceremony, setting the tone for the union. These scriptures are then interpreted and applied to the particular context of the wedding, taking into account the personal preferences of the bride, groom and their families. This interpretation of the sacred texts is often referred to as 'creative adaptation' and it is this that gives each wedding ceremony its own unique charm.

Before a wedding ceremony begins, the priest typically recites verses from the Hindu religious texts and a range of religious symbols are often used over the course of the event, such as the tilak mark on the forehead of the groom, and the turmeric paste present in many ceremonies. Flowers, incense and lamps are also often used to create a festive atmosphere and reflect an attitude of joy and reverence.

On the day of the wedding, the bride and groom exchange garlands and exchange small gifts. These gifts often have religious and spiritual connotations, such as souvenirs from temples, religious books and other items with religious symbolism. The wedding ceremony often takes place in a temple, where the couple are united in holy matrimony through a ritual called the Saptapadi, which involves the bride and groom each taking seven steps around a fire which is lit for the occasion, symbolizing the flame of love and commitment that binds them together.

After the Saptapadi, marriage is officially recognized and celebrated by singing, chanting and prayers. The entire ceremony reflects the significance and significance of religion in Indian culture and its importance in a successful marriage.

Religion clearly plays an important role in Indian weddings, both in terms of the ceremony itself and in the customs, rituals and religious symbols that regularly appears throughout the wedding and its accompanying events. This religious influence has been part of Indian weddings for centuries and is something that continues to this day, ensuring that each wedding is infused with the sacred and the traditional right from the very beginning.

"An Indian wedding is a beautiful mix of vibrant colours, exquisite decorations and joyous music."

෴

IX

The Role of Music and Dance in Indian Weddings

Music and dance are cornerstones of Indian weddings and have been for centuries. They bring together family and friends in an unforgettable atmosphere of joy and celebration. From pre-wedding celebrations to post-wedding ceremonies, music and dance play an integral role in Indian weddings.

Traditionally, pre-wedding celebrations are loud and spirited. The bride and groom's families come together to celebrate the pending union with feasts, singing, and dancing. Folk musicians perform Hindu devotional music, called Bhajans, and dance to lively bhangra beats, accompanied by drums and the occasional dhol. The elderly share tales about their families, and the young dance enthusiastically. These festivals are carried out in each family's native language and culture, adding unique depth to the event.

Post-wedding ceremonies are where music and dance really shine. From sangeet to baarat, music and dance fill the air with lively rhythms and joyful song. Before the bride and groom's initial meeting, curious family members and guests sing and dance in the Godh bharai ritual. In this ritual, the bride is welcomed with a barrage of singing and dancing, and showered with blessings.

Finally, after the bride and groom share their first glance and garlands, the groom arrives on an elaborately decorated horse or chariot. Family friends anoint the procession with enthusiastic performances. Some may dance traditional garbha steps, while others play the flute, shehnai, or tambourines to the beat of bhangra. These heartfelt expressions of joy accompany the groom to his wedding bed.

Finally, during the reception, music and dance take center stage. Dance floors are packed with guests eager to show off their moves. Professional dancers perform elaborate displays with pomp, color, and fanfare. Elsewhere friends and family break out into traditional dances, many of which contain intricate steps and colorful costumes. Throughout the evening, DJ's spin lively music to keep the party going.

At its best, music and dance bring together family and friends in a spirit of joy, celebration, and love. It can take many forms-- passionate, soothing, energetic, and so much more. It bridges gaps between cultures, generations, and languages. Ultimately, music and dance bring to life the rich diversity and beauty of an Indian wedding.

"An Indian wedding is a beautiful
amalgamation of vibrant traditions, joyous
customs and sheer happiness."

છ

X

The Attire of the Bride and Groom

The attire of the bride and groom is a very important aspect of an Indian wedding. It is a reflection of their beliefs and culture, which is why both the bride and groom must take great thought in their choice of clothing and jewellery.In Hindu weddings, the bride and groom are expected to wear the traditional Indian wedding clothes that include the sari and the sherwani.

When it comes to the bride, she will typically wear an exquisite red or pink sari. She can drape the sari in a traditional way or she can choose to use the contemporary style, where the pallu is draped over the left shoulder or over the head. Her sari is likely to be adorned with intricate zari work, intricate embroidery, elaborate sequin work or decorative borders. She will accessorise her sari with jewellery such as a maang tikka, nathiya, kamarbandh and a nose ring, among other traditional ornaments.

The groom is expected to wear a formal sherwani and either a matching turban or a bandhani safa. The sherwani can be made of silk, velvet, cotton or linen and it is typically richly embroidered with zari or threadwork, or it can be embellished with precious stones. The groom's outfit is often paired with detailed woven pattern jute mojari or leather juttis and a colourful pocket square. The groom usually finishes off his look with a nath, a kalgi and other traditional ornaments such as a mala and kamarbandh. The groom's jewellery is typically made of gold or silver.

The bride and groom's attire at an Indian wedding is not just about looking their best - it is about representing their culture and beliefs to the world. Most brides and grooms take considerable care and time in choosing their wedding attire, so that they make a strong statement on the most important day of their lives.

"An Indian wedding is more than just a joining of two souls, but a union of two cultures."

XI

The Food and Feast of Indian Weddings

Indian weddings are renowned for their grandeur and lavishness. From the décor to the clothes, the weddings not only exude ornateness and splendor but also for the scrumptious feast and lip-smacking food. No wedding dinner is complete without tantalizing delicacies that rejoice and tantalize the taste buds of the guests.

At the center of Indian wedding festivities is the grand dinner. Indian weddings feature some of the most delicious cuisines from different parts of the country. Most of the dishes revolve around the use of multi colored spices and flavors. The dinner usually has a combination of traditional and contemporary dishes that are sure to whet the appetite of even the biggest foodie. The buffet table is usually lined with exotic starters such as vegetable pakoras, samosas, tikkis, tandoori items and kebabs.

The main course dishes include a delectable selection of mouthwatering deliciousness. This usually includes several colors and tastes of dal, along with some exotic vegetables, a wide choice of Paneer (cottage cheese) items, chicken and mutton curries, fish, biryani and a variety of naans and rotis. For desserts, barfis, jalebis, gulab jamuns, shahi tukda and many more sweet delicacies are prepared for the guests along with a variety of fruits. Ultimately, the dinner can be customized according to one's preference and budget.

In addition to the delicious food, the dinner is also accompanied by a wide selection of drinks. The assortment of drinks may include soft drinks, milkshakes, lassi and other drinks like Chaas. Alcoholic beverages often include beer, whisky and rum. Delicious mocktails, smoothies and juices are also served to ensure that people of all ages have something to sip on.

To add the icing on the cake, Indian weddings usually feature a local band or musical performers that provide upbeat and soulful background music to entertain the guests.

All in all, no Indian wedding is complete without the grand dinner. The delicious food and beverages, along with the music and entertainment makes it an alluring and engaging affair. The food and feast at Indian weddings is one of the most fundamental elements and it helps to create a great bond between friends and family.

"A wedding should be a celebration of love
and togetherness, just like an Indian
wedding."

ಹಲ

XII

The Indian Weddings in the Modern Era

Indian weddings have always been known for their elaborate and grand celebrations. With their distinct traditions, customs, and ceremonies, Indian weddings have captured the imagination of people the world over. In recent years, however, Indian weddings have been experiencing a shift, as more and more couples are opting for modern styles and trends when it comes to their nuptials.

Today's Indian weddings are an intermingling of old and new, combining traditional practices and rituals with modern sensibilities. Many couples are choosing to incorporate aspects of the Western wedding style into their own special day, while still honoring their culture and heritage. One such instance of this is the use of a wedding planner to help execute the nuptials, as opposed to having the responsibility fall on the families of the bride and groom. This allows the event to be organized in a timely and professional manner.

Along with wedding planners, many contemporary Indian weddings also involve the use of technology and media. Photographers are making use of drones, as well as other high-tech equipment, to capture the moments and beauty of the celebration, while videos are often produced to capture all of the details of the wedding. Social media has also made an appearance at modern Indian weddings, as the use of hashtags and other platforms have become an integral part of the ceremony.

Another feature of modern Indian weddings is the number of guests in attendance. While in the past, weddings were attended by primarily family members and close friends, today entire communities may be present. Technology has enabled people to share the news of their upcoming nuptials with people all over the globe, and thus, be surrounded by those who love and celebrate them on their special day.

Finally, no modern Indian wedding is complete without the food. Gone are the days of single-course meals and set menus. Instead, couples are opting for a variety of cuisines and menu options, as well as work with catering services to create a unique and wonderful culinary experience.

Modern Indian weddings are truly a sight to behold, a combination of the ancient and the new that reflects the beauty of the culture today. Through their unique celebration of love, these couples are able to begin the next chapter of their lives with a meaningful and wonderful beginning.

"The special bond shared between the bride and the groom is what makes an Indian wedding so special."

೮

XIII
The Indian Destination Weddings

Destination weddings are increasingly becoming the latest trend in the wedding industry, particularly in India. The beautiful, romantic atmosphere of the Indian destination weddings is something that cannot be found at a regular wedding. Couples and their families have the opportunity to exchange their vows of everlasting love and devotion amidst the majestic beauty of nature as the backdrop.

Beautiful mountain ranges and serene beaches form an excellent venue for destination weddings. Be it Udaipur or Shimla, couples are able to share their love for each other amidst all the grandeur of these tourist destinations, making the ceremony all the more special. The exotic, romantic atmosphere of the resorts offers all the fun, frolic and musical entertainment that the family of the bride and groom look for.

Apart from being a popular and beautiful venue, destination weddings also provide numerous perks to the couple and their family. Apart from having the freedom to customize each aspect of the wedding to their own preferences and tastes, couples also save money in the long run. With the wedding expenses included in the package, couples are also able to get the best possible deals owing to the bulk discounts offered by the hotels.

The best part of the destination wedding experience is that the couple and their families get to enjoy the most special day in their life amidst a blissful and memorable atmosphere. It is not just the couple that benefit from the destination wedding experience, but also their guests. Everyone in attendance is free to explore the hidden gems of the region, as well as enjoy a variety of culinary delights on offer at the resort or the adjoining areas.

All in all, Indian destination weddings are a wonderful way for couples to exchange their vows of eternal love and happiness in gorgeous settings. With the cost effective packages offered by the resorts, the couple can have the dream wedding they have always wanted without having to break the bank. It also gives their guests the opportunity to enjoy the beauty and charm of the destination, making for an unforgettable family experience!

"The many rituals of an Indian wedding illustrate the culture, beauty and unity of the Indian culture."

৪৩

XIV

The Indian Wedding Planning and Industry

The Indian Wedding Planning and Industry is one of the growing sectors in the Indian economy. It is estimated to grow at a CAGR of 15-20% through 2020 and reach a market size of US$50-60 Billion. The sector's growth is being driven by a rising number of weddings, rising disposable incomes, and an increasing preference towards organized and professional services.

The Indian wedding industry is a complex and diverse system of vendors, services, and products that help to organize the wedding. From photography and caterers to decorators and makeup artists, there are a range of services that are essential for any large-scale wedding. In addition, the vendors that provide these services are highly dependent on the tastes and preferences of the couple getting married, which has resulted in an increased diversity in the services being offered.

The industry is heavily concentrated in the metropolitan and large cities of India such as Mumbai, Delhi, and Chennai. This is due to the large population base, higher disposable incomes and the greater number of vendors that have set up their business in these cities due to the better infrastructure and resources that they can access. However, the industry is slowly expanding to the other parts of India as well.

The biggest challenge that the industry faces is the lack of dedicated regulation and clarity in contractual laws. Most vendors and service providers in the industry are small businesses or freelancers and are not covered under the standard rules of contracts. This creates uncertainty while entering into agreements and also makes it difficult to enforce them if disputes arise.

Another challenge faced by the industry is the lack of access to capital and credit. Most of these small service providers are unable to access formal institutional channels for credit and have to rely on informal networks for taking care of their financial needs. This has the effect of curtailing their growth and reducing the scope of services that they can offer.

Despite these challenges, the Indian Wedding Planning and Industry is one of the fastest growing segments in the economy and is expected to be one of the key drivers of economic growth in the near future. The industry is a complex network of services, vendors and products that must be navigated carefully in order to ensure that the wedding is a success. The industry needs dedicated regulation and access to capital in order to ensure that it can continue to grow and expand.

"The deep traditions and intricate details make an Indian wedding full of picture-perfect moments."

☙

XV

The ongoing significance of Indian Weddings

Indian weddings are deeply rooted in the Indian culture and continue to reflect the richness of the culture today. A traditional Indian wedding is a unique event; it is a meaningful ritual that celebrates the union of two families, marks the transition of a young couple into adulthood, and brings the bride and groom closer to their respective families and communities.

Indian Weddings today have grown beyond being just a rite of passage or a celebration. They have come to represent the spirit of the culture and its magnanimity. The richness of the event reflects the show of generosity, togetherness, and unity that has been preserved in Indian culture.

From the decorations and food to the traditions and rituals, everything is the epitome of lavishness and luxury. Today, many Indian families combine traditional and modern elements in their wedding ceremony.

The vibrant decorations and colours of drapes and flowers bring the venue to life, while the intricate Mehndi designs adorn the hands of brides and make them look more beautiful and attractive. The event is further vitalized with music and dance, as people of all ages enjoy the festivities.

Barat, the procession of the groom and his relatives, is also a hugely popular part of the wedding and radiates the rich Indian culture prominently. The rituals such as intense chanting of Vedic mantras, sacrifice of a black goat for the longevity of the married couples and the Mendhi ceremony complete the entire event ceremoniously.

Indian weddings are not complete without the bond of matrimony. Marriages in India are mostly arranged marriages, wherein couples are united with their families' approval. It's a bond of togetherness and mutual understanding that binds a couple together and keeps them together in the hard times. This commitment is what makes Indian weddings special.

The ongoing significance of Indian weddings lies in the ideas of togetherness and joy that they bring to families and communities. Indian weddings not only bring two families together but also involve an overall celebration that brings in a lot of creativity and customization. The decorated venues, aromas of delectable delicacies, vibrant celebration and an overwhelming feeling of joy make Indian weddings a unique affair.

Indian weddings are unique and solemn events, which have become a veritable part of Indian culture today. The richness and diversity of the rituals and celebrations make Indian weddings the most preeminent of any cultural wedding. These weddings continue to bring immense joy, everlasting memories and strong bonds of unity in their wake. Thus, their ongoing significance can not be overstated.

When it comes to Indian weddings, sophistication and grandeur are always on full display. With its graceful rituals, intricate details, and their beautiful symbolism, an Indian wedding truly paints a picture of the Indian culture. With all the finery, decorations, and joy, they are truly some of the most beautiful celebrations. To help capture the spirit behind this majestic event, here are 15 short and unique quotes on Indian weddings.

Other Books Of The Author

1. The Moments When I Met God
2. Kashiyile Theertha Pathangal
3. GURU GYAN VANI
4. Abhiprerak Gita
5. ASSI SE JAIN GHAT TAK
6. Hopelessness of Arjuna
7. The Soul and It's True Nature
8. Sense of Action (Karma)
9. Action through Wisdom
10. Action through Wisdom
11. THEORY AND PRACTICAL OF EVERY ACTION
12. LOGICAL UNDERSTANDING OF THE SUPREME
13. THE IMPERISHABLE SUPREME
14. Yatra Nishadraj se Hanuman Ghat Tak
15. Yatra Karnatak Ghat se Raja Ghat Tak
16. Yatra Pandey Ghat se Prayagraj Ghat Tak
17. Yatra Ranjendra Prasad Ghat se Dattatreya Ghat Tak
18. YaatraSindhiya Ghat se Gwaliar Ghat Tak
19. Yatra Mangala Gauri Ghat se Hanuman Gadhi Ghat Tak
20. Yatra Gaay Ghat Se Nishad Ghat Tak
21. MAA GANGA, GHATEN EVM UTSAV
22. Ganga Arti Dev Deepavali evam Any Utsav
23. Potentials of Digitalized India
24. VEDIC CONSCIOUSNESS
25. A Brief Introduction to Vedic Science
26. Kashi ke Barah Jyotirling
27. IMPACT OF MOTIVATION
28. Let's have a Milky Way Journey
29. Color Therapy in a Nutshell

Contact

DR. JAGADEESH PILLAI

PhD in Vedic Science

Four Times Guinness World Record Holder

Winner of Mahatma Gandhi Vishwa Shanti Puraskar and
Global Peace Ambassador

Gemology, Astro & Vastu Consultant - Spiritual Counselor

Consultant for designing World Record Ideas

Efficient Tarot Card Reader

9839093003

myrichindia@gmail.com

drjagadeeshpillai@facebook

drjagadeeshpillai@instagram

jagadeeshpillai@youtube

www. JAGADEESHPILLAI.com

೫

|| LOKAHA SAMASTHAHA SUKHINO BHAVANTU ||

• 83 •